Waterproof QUEENSLAND FISH GUIDE

T0362874

by Frank Prokop

Illustrations by Trevor Hawkins
Rigs by Geoff Wilson

AMBERJACK

Scientific name: *Seriola dumerili.*

Description: A relatively large, fast swimming species mainly found in offshore waters in the vicinity of reefs or drop-offs. Sometimes confused with yellowtail kingfish, the amberjack has a dark blue to olive tail fin whereas the kingfish has a yellow tail fin.

The anal fin of the amberjack is darker in colour with a characteristic white edging. Differs from similar samson fish in having more rays in the dorsal fin (32 – 33) versus 23 – 25 for the samson fish. The samson fish also appears to have red teeth, due to blood engorged gums. The amberjack attains a weight of 36 kilograms.

BARRACUDA

Scientific name: *Sphyraena barracuda.* Also known as Great barracuda, giant barracuda, giant sea pike.

Description: The most remarkable feature of the barracuda is its fearsome teeth. There are two pairs of enlarged canines on the upper jaw and one pair of enlarged canines on the lower jaw. There are other large, backward pointing teeth in both jaws.

The body is long and cylindrical with approximately 18 grayish cross bands on the back above the lateral line. These bands on the back and the more heavy body differentiate the barracuda from the similar snook, which is generally found outside of the range of the barracuda. The barracuda reaches 1.8 m and nearly 25 kilograms.

BARRAMUNDI

Scientific name: *Lates calcarifer*. Also known as Barra, giant perch.

Description: The barramundi is a special fish which is as beautiful in reality as it is in the dreams of so many anglers. It has a small head with a large mouth and large eyes.

Barramundi have large scales and a particularly powerful tail. Coupled with their thick shoulders, barramundi can put up a good fight, many fish will exhibit the famous gill arching leaps when hooked.

The barramundi can be a brilliant silver colour for sea run fish, ranging to a very dark, chocolate brown colour for fish in billabongs at the end of the dry season or those grown in aquaculture facilities.

Small barra and those in aquaria exhibit a characteristic light stripe down the forehead between the eyes which becomes more pronounced when the fish is excited.

Barramundi in Australia change sex as they grow older (interestingly barramundi in Thailand do not change sex). All fish start out as males and, after spawning once or twice, become female for the rest of their lives. It is therefore impossible to catch a granddaddy barra as it would certainly be female. This sex change is more related to age than size, but barramundi over 8 kg are almost certainly all female.

Rigs and Tactics:

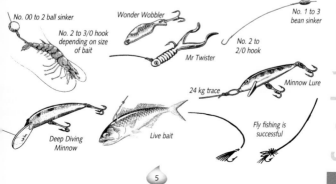

No. 00 to 2 ball sinker

No. 2 to 3/0 hook depending on size of bait

Wonder Wobbler

Mr Twister

No. 1 to 3 bean sinker

No. 2 to 2/0 hook

Minnow Lure

24 kg trace

Deep Diving Minnow

Live bait

Fly fishing is successful

saltwater Species

BASS, RED

POISONOUS

Scientific name: *Lutjanus bohar.*

Also known as Two spot red snapper, kelp bream, kelp sea perch.

Description: The red bass is a strikingly coloured fish which can be almost bright orange to a deep brick red. The scales have a paler centre which gives an attractive dappled effect. There is a diagnostic deep groove or channel (often described as a pit) which runs from the nostrils to the front of the eye. The presence of this groove distinguishes the red bass from the similar mangrove jack where larger specimens are also caught on offshore reefs. The snout of the red bass is somewhat pointed. The tail fin is slightly indented and the ventral and anal fins may have a white margin. There is a moderate notch in the preopercular bone. The red bass can reach 13 kg and a length of 90 centimetres.

BREAM, PIKEY

Scientific name: *Acanthopagrus berda* Also known as Bream.

Description: The pikey bream is very similar to the black bream, but with more pointed snout and very stout second anal spine. The pikey bream overlaps in range with the western and eastern yellowfin bream, both which possess yellow anal and caudal fins. The pikey bream also lacks the characteristic black spot at the base of the pectoral fin of the yellowfin bream. Attains a maximum size of 55 centimetres.

Fishing: Similar methods as for the black bream, but more common around jetties, pylons and creek mouths. The pikey bream makes excellent eating but should be bled and chilled after catpure.

6

BREAM, YELLOWFIN

Scientific name: *Acanthopagrus australis*.
Also known as Silver bream, sea bream, surf bream, Eastern black bream.

Description: The yellowfin bream is similar to other bream, but with a black spot at the base of the pectoral fin. Also has yellow or yellowish anal and ventral fins. Frequently taken from inshore oceanic waters where the colour is frequently silver, varying to dark olive from estuaries. Lacks the brown horizontal stripes and black stomach cavity lining of the similar tarwhine.

Attains a maximum size of 66 cm and 4.4 kg but fish over a kilogram are noteworthy.

CHINAMAN FISH

POISONOUS

Scientific name: *Symphorus nematophorus*. Also known as Threadfin sea perch (juveniles), galloper. Should not be confused with the Chinaman cod (*Epinephelus rivulatus*) which is a common and safe catch in northern Western Australia.

Description: Juveniles look substantially different from adults with blue stripes on a yellow background and extended soft dorsal ray filaments. Fins are reddish pink.

Adults lack extended filaments and are reddish with dark vertical bars. Adults have a stout body and a row of scales on the cheeks. The Chinaman fish also possesses a deep pit on the upper snout, immediately before the eyes.

CATFISH, FORKTAIL

Scientific name: *Arius graeffei*.
Also known as Salmon catfish, blue catfish, sea catfish.

Description: These catfish are quite remarkable in that the males hold the large eggs in their mouths until they hatch.

The various forktail catfish are difficult to differentiate. The giant salmon catfish (Arius leptaspis) grows to over 1.1 m as opposed to 69 cm for the blue catfish. The giant catfish has dorsal and pectoral spines which are the same length.

Fishing: Fork tailed catfish are held in low esteem by many anglers. This is largely as they are often taken while fishing for more prized species like barramundi, queenfish or mangrove jack, taking live baits or creating a false expectation when a lure is hit. Catfish will take baits and lures very well. They have a particular preference for cut baits.

Larger forktail catfish fight well and the eating qualities of catfish from clean water is higher than generally believed, as the market acceptance of silver cobbler will attest.

COBIA

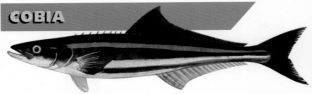

Scientific name: *Rachycentron canadus*. Also known as Cobe, black kingfish, black king, crab-eater, sergeant fish, lemon fish.

Description: A large pelagic species reaching over 2 m and 60 kilograms. Frequently mistaken initially for shark in the water due to its high dorsal fin and large, dark pectoral fins.

They have a relatively pointy head with the mouth at the middle of the front of the head. They have a white or creamy belly which tends to be darker around the anal fin region and a white stripe on their sides which may fade after death. They also have very short dorsal spines before the high soft dorsal fin. Other fins, except pelvic are dark and the overall colour is chocolate brown to black.

COD, BLACK

Scientific name: *Epinephelus daemelii*.
Also known as Saddled cod, saddled rock cod, saddletail cod.

Description: Found on offshore reefs, occasionally found in estuaries. Young fish are mottled grey with six vivid vertical bands. When fully grown they are capable of rapid colour changes, but retain a dark patch just above the tail. Grows to 45 kilograms.

COD, ESTUARY

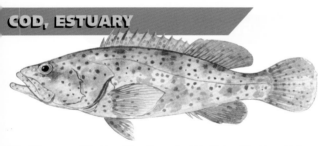

Scientific name: *Epinephelus coioides*. (Frequently misidentified as *Epinephelus malabaricus* or *Epinephelus tauvina*) Also known as Greasy cod, spotted cod, north-west groper, estuary rock cod, gold spotted rock cod, spotted river cod, orange-spotted cod.

Description: The estuary cod is one of the largest and most common cod found in tropical estuaries and coastal reefs reaching a length of over 2 m and 230 kilograms. The estuary cod is olive-green to brown with scattered brown spots. The back has four to six darker blotches which fade with age to uniform brown colour. Similar to Queensland groper but the estuary cod has three opercular spines equal distances apart. The tail is rounded.

COD, FLOWERY

Scientific name: *Epinephelus fuscoguttatus*. Also known as carpet cod, black rock-cod

Description: A heavy bodied cod species, the flowery cod generally has a fairly pale brown colour with darker chocolate brown 'flower' blotches on the sides. There are also numerous smaller spots over the body, including the stomach and the fins. The tail fin is heavily spotted and rounded.

Juvenile flowery cod up to around 4 kg are often found in northern mangrove creeks. Adults are found on offshore reefs or on broken ground near reefs. This species can reach 90 cm while the small toothed cod reaches 63 centimetres.

DART, SWALLOWTAIL

Scientific name: *Trachinotus botla*.

Also known as Dart, Common Dart, Swallowtail, Southern swallowtail.

Description: From the same family as trevally, the swallowtail dart bears some external similarities and shares the same tenacious side-on fight. Dart are handsome fish with a deeply forked tail. The dorsal fin is set well back on the fish and the first few dorsal and anal rays are elongated. The swallowtail dart has between one and five large spots on the side. The swallowtail dart is distinguished from the black spotted dart whose spots are smaller than the pupil of the eye. The snub nosed dart has no spots on its sides and a much more blunt, rounded head profile.

The swallowtail dart grows to 60 cm but is often caught at smaller sizes. Their strong fight makes up for their lack of size.

EMPEROR, BLUE SPOT

Scientific name: _Lethrinus laticaudis_.

Also known as grass emperor, grass sweetlip, coral bream, snapper bream, grey sweetlip, red-finned emperor, brown sweetlip.

Description: The various species of spangled emperors are difficult to differentiate. Many of the species have different size limits and must be able to be separated to comply with various state fishing regulations.

The blue spot emperor is a common capture in tropical waters and is often caught near weed beds. Juveniles in particular can be caught near beds of eel-grass (_Zostera sp._). The blue lined emperor grows to 80 cm. There are blue spots on the cheeks, as opposed to blue bars on the spangled emperor.

EMPEROR, LONG NOSED

Scientific name: _Lethrinus olivaceous_.

Description: One of the largest species of emperor, reaching 10 kg and a metre in length. The long nosed emperor is easily distinguished by the long sloping head and the generally greenish colouration. The long nose becomes readily apparent when compared to other similar species. There is generally a red line on the lips of these fish and the dorsal fin may have red spots.

Fishing: Standard reef fishing tackle and rigs will account for this hard fighting species. The long nosed emperor can be found on inshore or offshore reefs and its larger size can cause extra troubles for angling. Fresh baits and strong leaders are recommended for this species. Fish flesh, squid, octopus, pilchard or live baits are best. Highly regarded as a food fish.

Rigs and Tactics:

Bug sinker crimped to line

Linked No. 2/0 to 4/0 Limerick or Kendall Kirby hooks

Solid brass ring

Solid brass ring

30–40 cm No. 2/0 to 8/0 hook

60–120 g snapper sinker

No. 3/0 hook - Limerick, Suicide or Viking pattern

Dropper loop 30 cm

Main line

50 cm

Dropper loop 15 cm

50 cm 1/2 kg snapper sinker

Main line

No. 3/0 hook

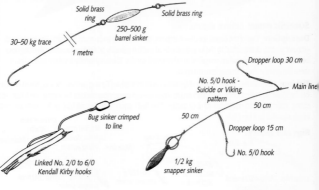

Scientific name: *Lutjanus sebae*. Also known as Government bream, red kelp.

Description: A striking and highly prized reef fish. The red emperor is a schooling fish which means that fishing can be fast and furious, but this valuable species can be taken in large numbers in commercial fish traps and trawls.

The red emperor changes appearance as it grows. Juveniles are known as Government bream as the three striking bands resemble a convict's broad arrow. This pattern fades with age and fish over 13 kg become a uniform scarlet or salmon pink. The reddish fins are narrowly edged with white. The cheeks are scaled and there is a deep notch in the lower edge of the pre-operculum (inner cheekbone).

Rigs and Tactics:

Solid brass ring
Solid brass ring
250–500 g barrel sinker
30–50 kg trace
1 metre

Dropper loop 30 cm
No. 5/0 hook - Suicide or Viking pattern
Main line
50 cm
50 cm
Dropper loop 15 cm
No. 5/0 hook

Bug sinker crimped to line
Linked No. 2/0 to 6/0 Kendall Kirby hooks
1/2 kg snapper sinker

EMPEROR, SPANGLED

Scientific name: *Lethrinus nebulosus.* Also known as Nor-west snapper, Nor'wester, yellow sweetlip, sand snapper, sand bream.

Description: A striking member of the sweetlip group. This species is easily identified by the blue spots on each scale and the blue bars on the cheek. This species can reach 86 cm and 6.5 kg and is considered very good eating.

Fishing: The spangled emperor is generally taken adjacent to coral or rock reefs over gravel or sand bottoms. They frequent lagoons and coral cays and can be taken from the beach in Western Australia where there are reef patches nearby. They are particularly active at night.

The spangled emperor can be taken with standard reef rigs, but as they are most common in water under 15 metres deep, lighter rigs and berley can bring these fish up into the open. Use cut fish, pilchards, squid, octopus, crab or prawn baits. Spangled emperor will take jigs or minnow lures either trolled or cast in areas near reefs where spangled emperor feed.

Rigs and Tactics:

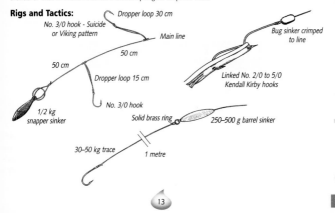

Dropper loop 30 cm

No. 3/0 hook - Suicide or Viking pattern

Main line

Bug sinker crimped to line

50 cm

50 cm

Dropper loop 15 cm

Linked No. 2/0 to 5/0 Kendall Kirby hooks

No. 3/0 hook

1/2 kg snapper sinker

Solid brass ring

250–500 g barrel sinker

30–50 kg trace

1 metre

Scientific name: *Lethrinus miniatus.*
(*formerly Lethrinus chrysostomus*) Also known as Sweetlip, lipper, red-throat, trumpeter (Norfolk Island)

Description: The sweetlip emperor is the most common of the emperor species, especially in Queensland. This species is identified by orange areas around the eyes, a bright red dorsal fin, and a red patch at the base of the pectoral fins. The inside of the mouth is red. Some fish have a series of brown vertical bands but many fish are a uniform colour. This species reaches a metre and 9 kg but is more common from 1 to 2.5 kilograms.

Fishing: Found in reef country, but frequently taken from areas between reefs, the sweetlip emperor can be berleyed up and large catches taken from the feeding school. The sweetlip emperor fights well and is able to dive to the bottom and break off an unwary angler.

These fish respond well to oily fleshed baits such as pilchard or mackerel, but when feeding can be caught on most baits including cut baits, squid, octopus, prawn and crab. Sweetlip emperor are highly regarded food fish.

Rigs and Tactics:

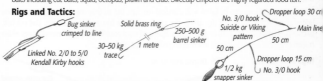

Scientific name: *Lutjanus johnii.* Also known as Fingermark bream, big scale red, golden snapper

Description: The fingermark is a large sea-perch commonly taken from northern inshore and reef waters and estuaries. It has a speckled appearance because of a dark spot on each scale, which give the appearance of parallel fine stripes. A large black blotch which varies in colour and intensity is located below the soft dorsal rays. Grows to 90 cm and more than 10 kilograms.

Saltwater Species

FLATHEAD, BAR-TAIL

Scientific name: *Platycephalus endrachtensis*. Also known as Western estuary flathead.

Description: The bar tail flathead can be readily identified by the tail fin which has black and white horizontal stripes on the tail with a yellow blotch at the top of the fin. The similar northern sand flathead which grows to 45 cm has similar tail colouration but no yellow blotch. The bar-tail flathead is found on sand, gravel, light rock and silt bottoms.

The bar-tailed flathead is reported as reaching 1 m in length, but in the Swan estuary where it is particularly targeted, any fish above 55 cm is noteworthy and most fish are between 30 and 45 centimetres.

FLATHEAD, SAND

Scientific name: *Platycephalus arenarius* (Northern sand flathead), Platycephalus bassensis (Southern sand flathead) Also known as Northern-flag tailed flathead; Southern - slimy flathead, bay flathead, common flathead, sandy flathead.

Description: The northern sand flathead can reach 45 cm but is more commonly encountered in large numbers at around 30 cm in estuaries or on adjacent beaches. They can be found to a depth of 30 fathoms. They have a distinctive pattern of long, horizontal black stripes the tail. This species is reputed to reach over 3 kg but is rarely found over a kilogram.

Fishing: The northern sand flathead will move upwards a greater distance to take a lure than the other flathead. These fish can be a pest at smaller sizes, seemingly being all mouth and spines and picking apart baits intended for other fish. They are good eating and are undervalued.

FLATHEAD, DUSKY

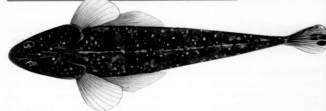

Scientific name: *Platycephalus fuscus*. Also known as Estuary flathead, mud flathead, black flathead, flattie, frog and lizard (especially large specimens).

Description: The dusky flathead is the largest of the 30 species of flathead in Australia, reaching 10 kg and 150 centimetres. Any fish above 5 kg is certainly worth boasting about. The flathead shape is unmistakable, and the dusky flathead also has the sharp opercular (cheek) spines to spike the unwary. The colouration is highly variable from light fawn to black depending on the type of bottom they are found on. The belly ranges from creamy yellow to white.

The tail fin features a characteristic dark spot in the top end corner and a patch of blue on the lower half. This is an estuarine or inshore species. This feature plus its large size and good eating make it the ultimate prize for many weekend anglers.

Rig and Tactics:

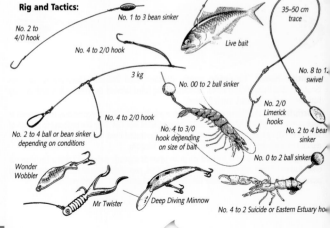

No. 2 to 4/0 hook

No. 1 to 3 bean sinker

No. 4 to 2/0 hook

Live bait

35–50 cm trace

No. 8 to 1. swivel

3 kg

No. 00 to 2 ball sinker

No. 2/0 Limerick hooks

No. 4 to 2/0 hook

No. 2 to 4 ball or bean sinker depending on conditions

No. 4 to 3/0 hook depending on size of bait

No. 2 to 4 bean sinker

No. 0 to 2 ball sinker

Wonder Wobbler

Mr Twister

Deep Diving Minnow

No. 4 to 2 Suicide or Eastern Estuary hook

JAVELIN FISH, SPOTTED

Scientific name: *Pomadasys kaakan.*
Also known as Spotted grunter-bream, grunter.

Description: The spotted javelin fish possesses black spots between the prominent spines of the dorsal fin, but these are much reduced in adult fish. The anal spine is prominent, giving rise to the name javelin fish. These fish grind their sharp pharyngeal (throat) teeth which is amplified by the fish's swim bladder. They are commonly found at the mouths of mangrove creeks and off rocky foreshores. They can reach 66 cm and 4.5 kilograms.

Fishing: The javelin fish feeds on prawns, crabs, worms, small fish and squid. The javelin fish will often run with the bait before taking it into their mouths. Therefore running sinkers and relatively light line at 4 – 6 kg is an advantage. The javelin fish can be caught on minnow lures and jigs. Javelin fish are a fine table fish which can be frozen at no cost to quality.

JEWFISH, BLACK

Scientific name: *Protonibea diacanthus.* Also known as Black jew, Spotted croaker, Spotted jew, Blotched jewfish, black mulloway, northern mulloway.

Description: The black mulloway is a large and prized northern mulloway species, growing to 40 kg and more than 1.5 metres. The range is important as there are few locations where black jewfish and mulloway can be taken together. The black jewfish has two prominent anal spines whereas the mulloway has a small second anal spine. The soft dorsal fin has 22 to 25 rays as opposed to 28 to 31 rays for the smaller and lighter coloured silver jewfish (*Nibea soldado*) of north-eastern waters which also has white ventral fins. The black jewfish has a grey to blackish colour. Young fish have black spots on the back, dorsal and tail fins.

Rigs and Tactics:

Live bait
Deep Diving Minnow
30–50 kg trace
Solid brass ring
1 metre
Solid brass ring
250–500 g barrel sinker

35–50 cm trace
No. 8 to 12 swivel
No. 2/0 to 8/0 hooks
No. 2 to 4 bean sinker

KINGFISH, YELLOWTAIL

Scientific name: *Seriola lalandi*. Also known as Kingie, yellowtail, hoodlum and bandit.

Description: The yellowtail kingfish is a beautiful, powerful fish which has a large, deeply forked tail. The back and upper sides are dark, purply blue while the lower part of the body is white. These two distinctive colours are separated by a yellow band which varies in width and intensity from fish to fish. The tail is a bright yellow. This can be a large fish reaching 2 m and more than 50 kg although increasing commercial and recreational fishing is affecting the presence of large fish. Any yellowtail kingfish over 20 kg will be a memorable capture.

Fishing: The yellowtail kingfish is a brutal, dirty fighter which will fully test the skill of the angler and the quality of their gear. The first run of a kingfish is straight towards the nearest bottom obstruction to cut off an unwary angler. Kingfish will take a wide variety of lures such as minnow lures, soft plastics and and flies. Vertical jigging with metail lures can be deadly at times. They will take a range of whole and cut fish baits, prawns, squid, octopus and cuttlefish but there are occasions when they can be finicky. At other times yellowtail kingfish will strike at bare hooks. Live bait is almost certain to attract a mad rush from any kingfish in the area.

Kingfish were previously considered average eating, but they have been increasingly recognised as a quality fish, including as sashimi. Large fish are worse eating and can have worms in the flesh, especially from northern waters.

Rigs and Tactics:

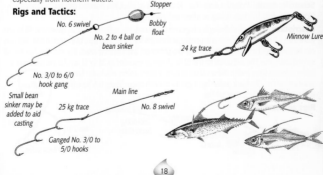

LONGTOM, SLENDER

Scientific name: *Stronylura leiura*. Also known as common longtom

Description: The slender longtom is a slender and sleek species. It is most easily separated from other longtoms by the bar along the base of the gill cover which can fade after death. The tail fin is square or may be convex. The jaws are elongated, fine and filled with needle sharp teeth.

The slender longtom is most commonly found in coastal waters and can be found in large bays and estuaries. This species can reach 110 cm but is most frequently encountered in estuaries at a smaller size.

MACKEREL, FRIGATE

Scientific name: *Auxis thazard*. Also known as Little tuna.

Description: A handsome fish which can reach 60 cm and around 5 kilograms. The frigate mackerel possesses the distinctive broken oblique lines above the lateral line and no markings below the lateral line. It can be easily separated from the similar mackerel tuna as the frigate mackerel has a wide gap between the two dorsal fins, no black spots near the ventral fins and a more slender body. The frigate mackerel can form large shoals in coastal or inshore waters.

Rigs and Tactics:

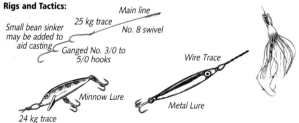

Small bean sinker may be added to aid casting

25 kg trace

Main line

No. 8 swivel

Ganged No. 3/0 to 5/0 hooks

Wire Trace

Minnow Lure

24 kg trace

Metal Lure

MACKEREL, BROAD-BARRED SPANISH

Scientific name: *Scomberomorus semifasciatus*. Also known as Grey mackerel, tiger mackerel, broad barred mackerel.

Description: A similar species to the more common and generally larger Spanish mackerel, they can be readily identified by the much larger soft dorsal and anal fins. The bars are much broader and fewer in number with live fish, but they fade significantly on death, giving rise to the marketing name of grey mackerel. The broad-barred Spanish mackerel reaches 1.2 m and 8 kg but is commonly caught at 1 – 3 kg from inshore waters or major embayments such as Tin Can Bay in Queensland.

Fishing: Like its larger cousin, the broad-barred Spanish mackerel readily takes small minnow or chrome lures and whole or cut fish baits. Live baits work extremely well. This species fights well, particularly on light line but is not as highly regarded a food fish as the Spanish mackerel.

Rigs and Tactics:

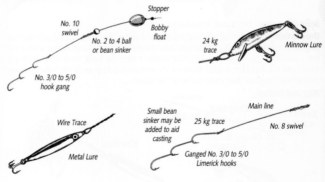

Stopper

Bobby float

No. 10 swivel

No. 2 to 4 ball or bean sinker

No. 3/0 to 5/0 hook gang

24 kg trace

Minnow Lure

Wire Trace

Metal Lure

Small bean sinker may be added to aid casting

25 kg trace

Main line

No. 8 swivel

Ganged No. 3/0 to 5/0 Limerick hooks

MACKEREL, QUEENSLAND SCHOOL

Scientific name: *Scomberomorus queenslandicus*. Also known as School mackerel, doggie mackerel, blotched mackerel, shiny mackerel.

Description: The Queensland school mackerel is a schooling species which frequents inshore areas. The Queensland school mackerel can reach a metre in length and a weight of 12 kilograms. However they are commonly encountered from 1.5 to 4 kg, especially on the eastern seaboard. This species is easily identified by the large dark spots on the sides and the black then white areas on the first dorsal fin. The pectoral fin is also smaller and more pointed than in the broad-barred Spanish mackerel.

Fishing: Schools of Queensland school mackerel can be berleyed close to the boat and taken with live or whole dead or fresh cut bait. These fish will take lures but can be finicky. Queensland school mackerel can patrol close to the shore and can be a surprise catch from tropical beaches or creek mouths, but they can bite off lures or baits intended for other species. The Queensland school mackerel is a top table fish if filleted.

Rigs and Tactics:

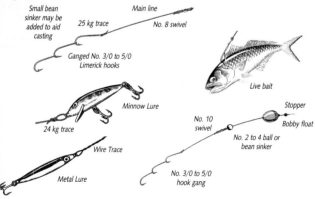

Small bean sinker may be added to aid casting

Main line

25 kg trace

No. 8 swivel

Ganged No. 3/0 to 5/0 Limerick hooks

Minnow Lure

24 kg trace

Wire Trace

Metal Lure

Live bait

Stopper

Bobby float

No. 10 swivel

No. 2 to 4 ball or bean sinker

No. 3/0 to 5/0 hook gang

MACKEREL, SHARK

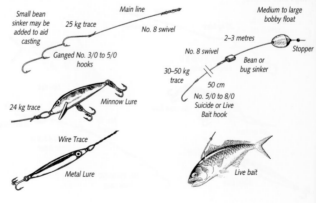

Scientific name: *Grammatorcynus bicarinatus*.

Also known as Scaly mackerel, large-scaled tunny, salmon mackerel.

Description: A sought after fish found on shallow reef areas throughout its range. This species has a distinguishing double lateral line which divides at the pectoral fin and joins again at the tail base. The belly displays dark spots and the eye is relatively small, especially compared to the similar double lined (or scad) mackerel. The scales of the shark mackerel come away in large sheets.

The name shark mackerel comes from a distinctive ammonia smell (shark-like) when the fish is cleaned but which disappears with cooking. The shark mackerel can reach 1.3 m and 11 kilograms.

Fishing: Shark mackerel are good lure prospects, rising to take minnow or spoon type lure where they put up a determined surface based fight. Shark mackerel are also taken on drifted whole or cut fish baits and live baits, although shark mackerel are not the general target species with live baits in tropical waters. The shark mackerel makes reasonable eating but the quality is improved by skinning the fillets.

Rigs and Tactics:

Small bean sinker may be added to aid casting

25 kg trace

Main line

No. 8 swivel

Ganged No. 3/0 to 5/0 hooks

Medium to large bobby float

2–3 metres

Stopper

No. 8 swivel

Bean or bug sinker

30–50 kg trace

50 cm

No. 5/0 to 8/0 Suicide or Live Bait hook

24 kg trace

Minnow Lure

Wire Trace

Metal Lure

Live bait

22

MACKEREL, SPANISH

Scientific name: *Scomberomorus commerson*. Also known as Narrow-barred Spanish mackerel, blue mackerel, tanguigue, Spaniard, seer, seerfish.

Description: The Spanish mackerel is a highly sought after and valued species capable of reaching 2.35 m and 42 kilograms. It is commonly taken from 5 – 15 kilograms. Smaller fish travel in pods of similar sized fish. The Spanish mackerel is similar to the wahoo but has fewer dorsal spines (15 – 18 versus 23 – 27) in a shorter dorsal fin. The upper jaw of the Spanish mackerel has an obvious external bone which extends to at least the middle of the eye, while in the wahoo there is no obvious bone and the upper jaw extends to the front edge of the eye. The Spanish mackerel is found in coastal waters, frequently in the vicinity of reefs.

Fishing: Spanish mackerel will aggressively take trolled lures and baits. Minnow lures, spoons and feathered lures run at 5 – 7 knots work best, while trolled garfish, slimy mackerel or other fish at 3 – 5 knots will take good catches. Spanish mackerel will also take drifted live, whole or cut baits. Land based fishermen drift large baits under balloons to take large fish. A wire trace can be an effective counter to the sharp teeth of the Spanish mackerel.

The Spanish mackerel is an excellent sport fish, particularly on light line, as it runs strongly and occasionally jumps in its attempts to escape. Spanish mackerel can actively feed at different depths, so lures and baits which target a wide range will more quickly locate fish.

The Spanish mackerel is a highly regarded food fish, but does not freeze particularly well, especially if cut into steaks. The quality is much better when the fish is filleted.

Rigs and tactics:

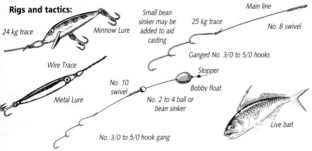

24 kg trace   Minnow Lure

Small bean sinker may be added to aid casting

Main line

25 kg trace   No. 8 swivel

Ganged No. 3/0 to 5/0 hooks

Wire Trace

Metal Lure

No. 10 swivel

Stopper

Bobby float

No. 2 to 4 ball or bean sinker

No. 3/0 to 5/0 hook gang

Live bait

MAHI MAHI

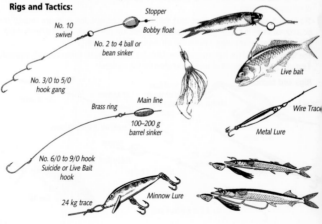

Scientific name: *Coryphaena hippurus*. Also known as Dolphin, dolphin fish, common dolphinfish, dorado

Description: The mahi mahi is one of the most beautiful fish in the ocean when lit up, with bright yellow to blue colouration and brilliant blue flecks over most of the body and fins. The fantastic colours fade to a washed out grey after death. Mature male or 'bull' mahi mahi have a prominent high forehead and tend to be more brightly coloured. Females have a more streamlined head profile.

The species is easily recognised in photographs due to its shape and brilliant colours. Other diagnostic features include the very long dorsal and anal fins and the deeply veed tail.

Mahi mahi are arguably the fastest growing species in the ocean, growing as much as a centimetre a day when food is plentiful. Mahi mahi can reach 2 m and more than 20 kg but are frequently taken in Australia from 2 to 10 kilograms. In Western Australia, mahi mahi are first found in oceanic waters at less than a kilogram and within five months, those that have not been caught are more than 10 kilograms.

Rigs and Tactics:

Stopper

Bobby float

No. 10 swivel

No. 2 to 4 ball or bean sinker

No. 3/0 to 5/0 hook gang

Live bait

Brass ring

Main line

100–200 g barrel sinker

Wire Trace

Metal Lure

No. 6/0 to 9/0 hook
Suicide or Live Bait hook

24 kg trace

Minnow Lure

MANGROVE JACK

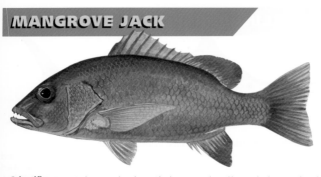

Scientific name: *Lutjanus argentimaculatus*.. Also known as Jacks, red bream, dog bream, red perch, reef red bream, purple sea perch, creek red bream.

Description: The mangrove jack is best known for its destruction of fishing tackle in tidal creeks, but these tend to be juvenile or small adult fish. The largest specimens are taken on offshore reefs to a depth of 100 metres. Mangrove jack can reach more than 1.2 m and a weight of 15 kg but fish in inshore waters are a real handful at 1 – 3 kilograms.

The mangrove jack is often confused with the red bass, which is a much more notorious ciguatera species, especially if caught on reefs. The mangrove jack has a taller dorsal fin, a lack of lengthwise stripes on its side and the absence of black on the fins. Mangrove jacks lack the distinctive pit before the eye of the red bass which is predominantly a coral reef species.

Rigs and Tactics:

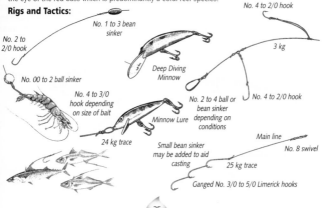

saltwater species

MARLIN, BLACK

Scientific name: *Makaira indica*. Also known as Giant black marlin, silver marlin.

Description: A magnificent blue water billfish capable of reaching a length of nearly 5 m and 850 kilograms. The black marlin is readily distinguished by its rigid pectoral fins which cannot be laid next to body in any black marlin and are completely rigid in all fish over 50 kg. In this fairly heavy bodied fish, the start of the second dorsal is forward to the start of the second anal fin. Black marlin are most commonly found in blue water, with many fish moving southwards with the warmer currents. Black marlin are found near current lines and where baitfish aggregations are prevalent.

Fishing: The black marlin is widely recognised as the most highly prized gamefishing species. The most famous fishing ground is off Cairns, where the future of grander marlin (over 1000 pounds) has been enhanced by the almost exclusive use of tag and release fishing and the recent establishment of this species as recreational only in Australia's 200 mile Exclusive Economic Zone. Black marlin are targeted by gamefishermen along most of the east and west coasts.

Black marlin are caught on trolled live and dead bait or less frequently on bait fished from a stationery boat. Marlin are also taken on trolled lures which consist of a hard moulded plastic or resin head and soft plastic skirt which travels just at or below the surface and leaves a bubble trail. Black marlin are a fast swimming pelagic species which are trolled at speeds between six and ten knots. A few marlin are caught by land based game fishermen, but only where deep, clean water comes close to shore.

They are not regarded as a food fish and almost all recreationally landed fish are released.

Rigs and Tactics:

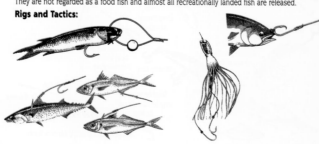

MULLET, SEA

Scientific name: *Mugil cephalus*.

Also known as Bully mullet, bully, mullet, hard-gut mullet, river mullet. Juveniles referred to as poddy mullet or poddies.

Description: The sea mullet is a cylindrical barrel of muscle which is readily identified by the thick, transparent, gelatinous covering over all but the centre of the eyes. They often have several diffuse lateral stripes on the side, but the colour and intensity can vary with the environment. Sea mullet have a distinguishing enlarged and pointed scale behind the top of the pectoral fin.

Sea mullet are found from far above the tidal reaches of coastal rivers to reasonable distances offshore, but they are best known for the vast shoals they can form at spawning time on east coast beaches. They are a very large species, reaching 80 cm and over 5 kg, but sea mullet are most commonly encountered at 1 – 2 kilograms.

Fishing: Sea mullet are almost exclusively vegetarian and as a result have to be enticed to be taken by recreational anglers, but they are worth the effort. There are few better fighters pound for pound in Australia and on light line, they really sizzle.

Sea mullet can be taken on flies and very rarely on accident with small lures but these are challenges beyond all but the most dedicated angler. Sea mullet are best targeted where effluent such as from fruit or vegetable factories, bakeries or flour mills enter the water. Here mullet are trained to take foods such as corn, pineapple or peas and are much easier to catch.

In other areas, it may take several days of berley in the same area and tide before sea mullet begin to bite freely. Best baits are dough or bread, prawn or worm pieces, generally fished on or just under the surface. Methods described for sand mullet work well. Patience is required, but well rewarded although in WA they remain almost impossible to catch.

Sea mullet are much better eating if taken from ocean beaches where they become hard-gut mullet, not eating but preparing for spawning. Unfortunately in the ocean larger fish are only taken through accidental foul hooking by recreational anglers. Estuarine fish (soft-gut mullet) can taste muddy or weedy and should be cleaned quickly. This poorer taste along with the high by-catch is another reason why commercial gill netting for mullet should be stopped in estuaries.

Rigs and Tactics:

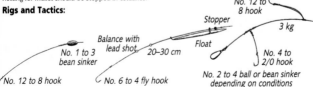

No. 1 to 3 bean sinker

Balance with lead shot

20–30 cm

Stopper

Float

No. 12 to 8 hook

No. 6 to 4 fly hook

No. 12 to 8 hook

3 kg

No. 4 to 2/0 hook

No. 2 to 4 ball or bean sinker depending on conditions

MULLOWAY

Scientific name: *Argyrosomus japonicus*. Also known as Jewfish, jew, jewie, butterfish, river kingfish, silver kingfish.

Small fish to around 3 kg are generally referred to as soapies due to their rather bland or soapy taste. Fish from 3 – 8 kg are frequently known as Schoolies as they are often encountered in schools which decrease in number as the size increases.

Description: Mulloway are a large and highly prized species found in estuaries, embayments and inshore ocean waters throughout its range. The mulloway can vary in colour from dark bronze to silver and there may be red or purple tinges, but a silver ocean mulloway is a stunning fish.

The mulloway has large scales and a generous mouth. A line of silvery spots follows the lateral line in live fish which glows under artificial lights as do the eyes which shine a bright red. A conspicuous black spot is just above the pectoral fin.

The tail fin is convex (rounded outwards) and this characteristic differentiates them from the smaller teraglin which has a concave tail and a yellow inside of the mouth.

Mulloway differ from the black jewfish which is generally darker with black blotches on the back and has a prominent second anal spine which is short in the mulloway.

Mulloway can reach 1.8 m and more than 60 kg, but any fish over 25 kg is worth long term boasting rights for the angler. Mulloway are most commonly caught at 3 – 10 kilograms.

Rigs and Tactics:

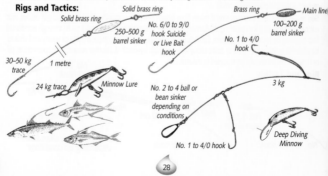

PARROTFISH

Scientific name: *Family Scaridae.*

Description: Closely related to the similarly colourful wrasses, parrotfish have their teeth fused into strong beak-like plates. Sexes can have different colours and juveniles often very different colours from adults.

Many parrotfish sleep in reef caves at night and can secrete a mucous envelope around their bodies while they rest. Sizes of parrotfish can range from the humphead parrotfish which can be up to 1.2 m to the more common green finned parrotfish which reaches 30 centimetres.

Fishing: Parrotfish are almost never taken by line fishermen, but some species can be important spearfishing targets. The surf parrotfish can be herded into shallows and captured by hand in some Queensland reefs.

The few parrotfish that are taken by line bite on prawn or worm baits intended for other species. Once hooked, the beak-like teeth can bite through lines and hooks. Parrotfish graze on live or dead corals or algae and can be important in the overall evolution of coral reefs. Parrotfish are highly regarded food fish but the bones are pale green.

PERCH, PEARL

Scientific name: *Glaucosoma scapulare.*

Also known as Pearly, nannygai.

Description: This is a handsome fish with a large eye and a large mouth. There is a small black spot at the base of the pectoral fin and a distinctive black flap of skin and bone near the top back edge of the gill cover.

A similar species, the deepsea or northern dhufish (Glaucosoma burgeri) is found from Onslow north and lacks the distinctive flap on the gill cover, has a bright silvery appearance and can reach 2.5 kilograms.

The pearl perch can reach 5 kg, but a fish over 3 kg is a quality fish.

Fishing: This is widely regarded as one of the best, if not the best eating fish on the east coast. Commercial and recreational overfishing has pushed these fish onto less heavily fished deep reefs in more than 50 m of water.

Pearl perch are frequently taken in conjunction with snapper and other deep water reef species, although they bite most freely at dusk and dawn. Heavy weights are necessary to reach bottom where pearl perch are found. Best baits are fresh cut baits, squid or cuttlefish with pilchards being a reliable standby.

PERCH, MOSES

Scientific name: *Lutjanus russelli.*

Also known as One spot sea perch, finger-mark (WA).

Description: Has a general reddish or pinkish hue, a large mouth with discernible canine teeth and 14 or 15 rays in the dorsal fin. The Moses perch has a distinctive black spot which can be quite pale, below the start of the soft dorsal rays. Most of the black spot is above the obvious lateral line, while the similar black-spot sea perch (*Lutjanus fulviflamma*) has a small black spot, most of which is below the lateral line. The lateral yellow stripes of the black-spot sea perch are not present on the Moses perch.

The Moses perch often forms schools of similar sized fish, hanging near coral outcrops and in eddies near reefs. They can be found near drop-offs, on reefs or in depths of up to 80 m, with larger specimens frequently captured from deeper water. The Moses perch reaches 50 cm and nearly 3 kg but is commonly caught at between 25 and 30 centimetres.

Fishing: Like many species in this group, the Moses perch can be an aggressive feeder, rising well to minnow lures, feather jigs and even surface poppers cast or trolled to the downstream side of coral outcrops. The school can jostle to be the first to take the lure or bait.

Baits include whole or cut fish baits, squid, octopus or prawns. Weights should be kept to a minimum, depending on the depth and mood of the fish, as Moses perch will rise to a bait which also puts them further from dangerous coral which they will try to use. In deeper water, lighter weights allow the fish to fight better and keeping the bait just above the bottom will deter some pickers but not Moses perch.

The Moses perch is a good eating fish.

Rigs and Tactics:

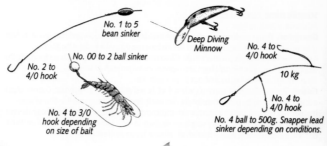

No. 1 to 5 bean sinker

Deep Diving Minnow

No. 4 to 4/0 hook

No. 00 to 2 ball sinker

No. 2 to 4/0 hook

No. 4 to 3/0 hook depending on size of bait

10 kg

No. 4 to 4/0 hook

No. 4 ball to 500g. Snapper lead sinker depending on conditions.

QUEENFISH

Scientific name: *Scomberoides commersonnianus*. Also known as Giant leatherskin, leatherskin, queenie, talang queenfish, skinny, skinnyfish.

Description: The queenfish is a large, long and laterally (side to side) compressed species which leads to the common name of skinny and a light weight for the length. The mouth is large and extends mouth well beyond the back of the eye whereas other smaller queenfish species have smaller mouths.

A series of 5 to 8 oval shaped blotches are found on the sides above the lateral line. The similar but smaller double spotted queenfish (*Scomberoides lysan*) has a double row of spots above and below the lateral line. The queenfish also has a prominent, high and light coloured front part of the dorsal and anal fins. These fish have lance shaped scales which are deeply embedded in a leathery skin.

The queenfish can reach 120 cm and more than 11 kilograms. This light weight for the length indicates how skinny the queenfish is when viewed head on.

Fishing: Queenfish are found from the upper tidal reaches of tropical rivers to inshore reefs and occasionally near outer reefs which have shallow breaks. Queenfish prefer slightly turbid water with plenty of flow. They are ambush feeders and will lurk near cover such as eddies, rock bars, wharves and creek mouths, especially on a falling tide.

Queenfish are spectacular and exciting sportfish, with their slashing strikes and blistering runs, often with aerial displays. Queenfish will take dead baits such as mullet, pilchard, garfish, mudskippers, whiting or fresh prawns and squid. They are also partial to live bait. Queenfish are renowned lure takers, with cast or trolled lures such as sliced chrome lures, spoons, shallow and deep diving minnows, spinner baits and surface lures. Queenfish are excited by escaping baitfish, so a fast, erratic retrieve is most successful. Fly enthusiasts are increasingly targeting queenfish as they are an exciting challenge on light fly gear. Large minnow type flies retrieved through current eddies on a fast strip works best. A heavy monofilament leader is recommended when fishing for queenfish as their jaws and small teeth can damage light traces.

Rigs and Tactics:

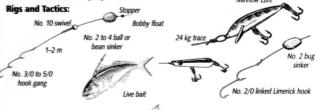

Minnow Lure

Stopper

No. 10 swivel

Bobby float

No. 2 to 4 ball or bean sinker

24 kg trace

1–2 m

No. 3/0 to 5/0 hook gang

Live bait

No. 2 bug sinker

No. 2/0 linked Limerick hook

saltwater species

SAILFISH, INDO-PACIFIC

Scientific name: _Istiophorus platypterus._ Also known as Pacific sailfish, bayonet fish, sailfish.

Description: The Indo-Pacific sailfish is most easily recognised by the prominent sail-like dorsal fin which forms the basis of the common name. The dorsal fin when lowered, fits into a groove. The shorter median dorsal rays are still longer than the body is deep. The characteristic upper jaw spear is slender and more than twice the length of the lower jaw. The ventral rays are very long and extend almost to the anus. The body and sail are spotted with dark and light blue. Stripes on the side may darken after death. Indo-Pacific sailfish can reach 120 kg, but any fish over 45 kg is a proud capture.

Fishing: The Indo-Pacific sailfish is a spectacular fish renowned for its spectacular leaps and strong surface runs. The sailfish is one of the smaller billfish but is highly prized, especially as a light line target. Sailfish can be taken by trolling live or dead baits of mullet, mackerel, garfish, rainbow runner or other common medium sized bait fish. Baits enhanced with plastic or feather skirts seem to take more fish. Many fish are taken on lures, including pusher or doorknob type lures or even minnow lures. Sailfish are becoming increasingly targeted with fly gear, as the use of teaser baits or lures can bring lit up sailfish within casting range and their spectacular fight makes them one of the ultimate targets for fly fishing aficionados.

Indo-Pacific sailfish are occasionally taken from rocky headlands adjacent to deeper water on drifted live baits or spincasting with baits or lures.

Australia, where even fairly small boats can encounter sailfish during peak periods.

Rigs and Tactics:

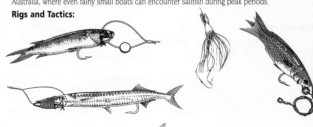

SALMON, COOKTOWN

Scientific name: *Eleutheronema tetradactylum*.

Also known as Threadfin, giant threadfin, blue salmon, Rockhampton kingfish.

Description: Even reliable reference books provide confusing information on the status of the various threadfin salmon species. The Cooktown salmon is the largest of these distinctive species which are easily identified by the unusual overshot upper jaw and absence of lips around a large mouth. The threadfin salmon species have an unusual body shape as the body is thickest through the second dorsal fin.

The most obvious diagnostic feature is the divided pectoral fin with its separate, finger-like filaments. The Cooktown salmon has four separate, and shorter pectoral filaments as opposed to five in the threadfin salmon.

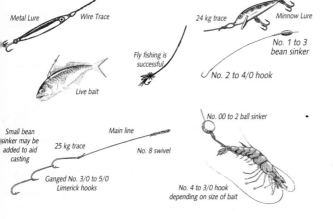

Metal Lure Wire Trace

Live bait

Fly fishing is successful

24 kg trace Minnow Lure

No. 1 to 3 bean sinker

No. 2 to 4/0 hook

Small bean sinker may be added to aid casting

25 kg trace Main line

No. 8 swivel

Ganged No. 3/0 to 5/0 Limerick hooks

No. 00 to 2 ball sinker

No. 4 to 3/0 hook depending on size of bait

saltwater Species

Scientific name: *Polydactylus sheridani*. Also known as Blue threadfin, blue salmon, Burnett salmon, king salmon.

Description: The threadfin salmon is similar to the Cooktown salmon, but possesses 5 long distinctive fingers on the lower edge of the pectoral fin. This species has a more pronounced blue colour and a long and relatively narrow caudal wrist. The threadfin salmon is common between 0.5 and around 3 kg with occasional specimens slightly larger.

Another similar species, the Northern or striped threadfin salmon (*Polydactylus plebius*) is separated by its more prominent stripes and overall golden colour and five free filaments, of which the two uppermost are longest.

Rigs and Tactics:

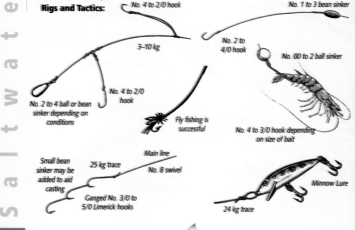

No. 4 to 2/0 hook

3–10 kg

No. 1 to 3 bean sinker

No. 2 to 4/0 hook

No. 00 to 2 ball sinker

No. 2 to 4 ball or bean sinker depending on conditions

No. 4 to 2/0 hook

Fly fishing is successful

No. 4 to 3/0 hook depending on size of bait

Small bean sinker may be added to aid casting

Main line

25 kg trace

No. 8 swivel

Ganged No. 3/0 to 5/0 Limerick hooks

Minnow Lure

24 kg trace

Saltwater Species

SHARK, BLACK TIPPED REEF

Scientific name: *Carcharhinus melanopterus*. Also known as blacktip, reef shark

Description: A small but easily identified whaler species reaching around 1.8 metres. The black-tipped reef shark has an obvious black tip to all of its fins, including both lobes of the tail. This is the only species with a black tip to the dorsal fin.

The black-tipped reef shark is found on reef country and is an active hunter. They will move up onto very shallow on a rising tide searching for food with their dorsal fins and even their backs scything through the water. They often travel in groups and can be quite disconcerting for swimmers or divers. They are considered to be one of the least dangerous of the whaler species, but caution should always be exercised, especially in groups of fish or where blood is in the water.

SHARK, HAMMERHEAD

Scientific name: *Sphyrna lewini*. Also known as Scalloped hammerhead shark.

Description: There is absolutely no mistaking the hammerhead shark, whose distinctive, broad head is unique.

The scalloped hammerhead shark can reach 6 m but is more common at around 3 metres. This species has a distinctive groove at the front edge of the hammer, which extends to the nostrils, which are near the eyes. They are common offshore, but can enter bays and inlets.

The smooth headed hammerhead lacks the distinctive groove or notch and reaches around 4 m in the colder water it prefers.

SHARK, MAKO

Scientific name: *Isurus oxyrinchus*. Also known as Shortfin mako, blue pointer, jumping shark.

Description: The mako shark is a sleek, beautifully streamlined close relative of the great white. The mako differs from the great white in being more streamlined and having distinctly pointed and hooked upper teeth as opposed to the distinctly triangular teeth in the great white . The mako is distinctly blue in colour though this fades to grey-blue after death. The pectoral fin is shorter than in the blue shark.

The mako prefers deep offshore waters, but can move into more coastal waters where its sleek form and hooked teeth make short work of any hooked fish. If the hooked fish is skull dragged past the mako, it can provoke an attack on the boat, leaving teeth in the hull and very shaken fishermen.

The mako is the most prized shark for game fishing, but is extremely dangerous for small boat fishermen.

Fishing: The mako shark is the most prized shark species for game fishermen. The strong fight and leaps of up to 6 m add to the excitement of taking these fish. Very good quality tackle is required and live or fresh dead fish baits will increase chances of a hook-up. The mako responds well to berley, especially near deep water current lines or schools of mackerel.

The mako is extremely dangerous for small boat fishermen as they can attack boats, jump into boats while still 'green', causing incredible damage, or even while seemingly dead they can muster energy to trash a small cockpit with slashing teeth and tail.

The mako is reasonable eating in small to medium sizes but should be bled and put on ice to prevent a build-up of ammonia in the flesh.

Rigs and Tactics:

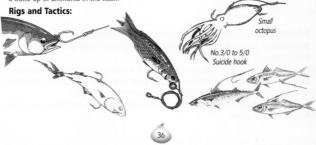

Small octopus

No.3/0 to 5/0 Suicide hook

SHARK, TIGER

Scientific name: *Galeocerdo cuvier.*

Description: A large and extremely dangerous species of shark. The tiger shark can be found well offshore and can venture into the surf zone on occasions, especially during breeding season. The characteristic colour pattern of the tiger shark is a tiger-like series of bars on the upper body. The teeth are unusually shaped, being large and pointed backwards, with strong serrations, especially on the back edge. Although the colouring and shape are distinctive, a dive charter at Ningaloo Reef, with a boat load of tourists, attempted to dive with a tiger shark they thought was a whale shark. The shark, like many when well fed and not threatened, was docile and there was no real incident.

The tiger shark can reach nearly 6.5 m and more than 600 kilograms.

Fishing: The tiger shark is a famous visitor to the old whaling stations of Australia, where large numbers of tigers, with a few great whites would attack whale carcasses waiting to be flensed.

Tiger sharks are attracted by berley and are taken with very large dead baits, especially those with oily or bloody flesh. The tiger shark is a powerful and dogged opponent and is sought by some specialist gamefishermen. Taking any large shark from small boats requires enormous preparation and should not be attempted by any inexperienced angler.

The tiger shark is a large and opportunistic feeder which will attack humans and should be treated with extreme caution. If sharks are not being targeted and a large tiger shark shows up – move.

Rigs and Tactics:

SNAPPER

Scientific name: *Pagrus auratus*. (formerly Chrysophrys auratus) Also known as schnapper, Pink snapper and pinkie. With increasing size known as Cockney bream, red bream, squire, snapper and ultimately 'old man snapper' with the characteristic hump.

Description: A truly stunning and highly sought after species, the snapper can have iridescent pink to burnished copper colouration with bright blue spots from the lateral line upwards which are brightest in younger fish. A hump on the head and nose area develops in some fish and is more likely in male fish. Snapper are relatively slow growing and mature at 29 to 35 cm and four to five years of age. Snapper numbers have been affected by both commercial and recreational overfishing.

Fishing: Snapper are traditionally taken on bottom paternoster rigs with the famous snapper lead. Snapper prefer the edges of reefs or broken ground and can be taken from the shore or as deep as 50 fathoms. Drifting over broken ground or drop-offs at the edges of reefs with just enough weight to bounce bottom will find fish and repeated drifts will pick up more fish. Like many reef species, snapper form schools of similar sized fish, with the size of the school decreasing with larger fish.

In late winter on the east coast, snapper move inshore to feed on spawning cuttlefish and large fish can be taken from the rocks on cuttlefish baits.

Quality snapper can be taken by sinking a bait under a feeding school of tailor, salmon or small mackerel, feeding on uneaten baitfish. Snapper are a magnificent fighting fish and are excellent eating, but do not freeze particularly well.

Rigs and Tactics:

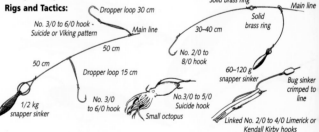

Dropper loop 30 cm

No. 3/0 to 6/0 hook - Suicide or Viking pattern

Main line

50 cm

50 cm

Dropper loop 15 cm

1/2 kg snapper sinker

No. 3/0 to 6/0 hook

Solid brass ring

Main line

Solid brass ring

30–40 cm

No. 2/0 to 8/0 hook

60–120 g snapper sinker

Bug sinker crimped to line

Linked No. 2/0 to 4/0 Limerick or Kendall Kirby hooks

No.3/0 to 5/0 Suicide hook

Small octopus

TAILOR

Scientific name: *Pomatomus saltatrix*. Also known as Tailer, chopper, bluefish (USA), elf (South Africa), skipjack.

Description: The tailor is a renowned predatory species best known for its relatively small but extremely sharp teeth. The tailor has a moderately forked tail, and a bluish to blue-green back which changes to more silvery and white on the belly. The eye can be yellow. The fins vary in colour but the tail fin is usually darker than the others.

Juvenile tailor are found in estuaries and embayments. Larger tailor move to the beaches and inshore reefs at between 25 – 35 centimetres. Tailor undergo a spawning migration, finishing at Fraser Island in Queensland and possibly the Abrolhos Islands in Western Australia, although the largest fish are most commonly found in Shark Bay. Tailor can reach 10 kg with any fish over 5 kg being rightly claimed as a prize and fish over 1.5 kg being large. Tailor are voracious feeders, with individual fish gorging themselves before regurgitating to continue in a feeding frenzy.

Fishing: Tailor are a highly prized species which readily takes a bait, fights hard and, if bled immediately after capture make fine eating. Tailor can be taken from boat or shore, on lure, fly or bait and by anglers of any skill level.

The most common bait and rig would be a whole pilchard bait on a gang hook rig. In the surf and where casting distance is required, a sliding sinker rig works best, with a star or spoon sinker on a dropper trace doing well. In estuaries, from a boat, or in calmer surf, an unweighted or minimally weighted bait provides by far the best results. Tailor readily feed high in the water column and avidly attack a floating bait. Another rig which works well is to use a nearly filled plastic bubble to gain casting distance without rapidly sinking the bait. Tailor bite best at dusk and dawn.

Tailor smoke very well and are fair eating when fresh which is improved if fish are immediately bled. The flesh of the tailor is fairly oily and bruises easily. Tailor makes a quality cut bait.

Rigs and Tactics:

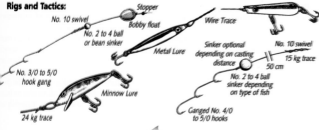

TARPON

Scientific name: *Megalops cyprinoides*. Also known as Oxeye herring.

Description: The tarpon is most easily identified by the long trailing filament at the rear of the single dorsal fin. The eye is also very large as are the upper jaw bones. The tail is deeply forked and powerful. The scales are very large.

Tarpon are commonly found in mangrove creeks, larger estuaries and bays. The tarpon can grow to 1.5 m and around 3.5 kilograms.

Fishing: The tarpon will take dead fish bait but can be very finicky. They can sometimes be taken on small live baits. Tarpon are a fantastic fighting fish for lure and fly fishers using small white jigs, small chrome lures and flies. The mouth of the tarpon is bony and hooks should be at their sharpest to get a hookup that can survive the strong fight and aerial display of the tarpon.

Tarpon are extremely bony and are poor eating. Care should be taken with handling to improve survival of released fish.

TRIGGERFISH, STARRY

Scientific name: *Abalistes stellaris*.

Description: The triggerfish are similar to the leatherjackets but differ in two obvious features. Triggerfish have three obvious dorsal spines in the first dorsal while leatherjackets have two of which the second is only rudimentary. Triggerfish also have obvious scales whereas leatherjackets have rough skin without obvious scales.

The starry triggerfish is one of the largest triggerfish species, reaching 60 centimetres. It is the triggerfish most frequently taken by recreational anglers. The mouth is small in the large head. The colour is pale and the common name comes from three white blotches on the back and a scattering of white spots on the upper body. There are yellow spots on the lower body. There are two small trailing filaments on both lobes of the tail in adults.

Fishing: This species is not a target species but is taken by line fishers, mainly in tropical reef areas. The small mouth means that small or long shanked hooks improve catch rates. Best baits are prawns, crab, squid or cut baits. Triggerfish are often regarded as a pest due to their ability to steal baits and avoid hook-ups. Triggerfish are reasonable eating but should be skinned.

TARWHINE

Scientific name: *Rhabdosargus sarba*. Also known as Silver bream.

Description: The tarwhine is similar to the various bream species but differs having a number of thin golden or brown stripes running the length of the silver body. The nose of the tarwhine is blunt and there are 11 or 12 anal rays whereas bream have 9 or fewer. The fins other than the dorsal fin are generally bright yellow or yellow-orange and it has a black lining to its gut cavity.

Tarwhine are common in inshore and estuarine areas and may be found on offshore reefs on occasions. Tarwhine form schools, especially in smaller sizes. Tarwhine can reach 80 cm and more than 3 kg but they are most commonly caught at a few hundred grams.

TREVALLY, BRASSY

Scientific name: *Caranx papuensis*. Also known as Papuan trevally.

Description: The brassy trevally is a very similar species to the giant trevally and is often misdescribed in fishing publications. The brassy trevally is often in schools of similar sized fish on inshore tidal areas or reef edges where they they often ambush feed. The brassy trevally has a white rear border to the lower lobe of the tail fin and sometimes the rear of the anal fin which separates it from the giant trevally. Both dorsal fins are dusky coloured and other fins have a yellow tinge or are yellow. Very small dark or black spots are often found on the upper half of the body. The brassy tinge to the overall body colour gives rise to the common name.

This species grows to around 80 cm, while the giant trevally can reach 1.7 metres.

TREVALLY, BIGEYE

Scientific name: *Caranx sexfasciatus*. Also known as Great trevally.

Description: Positive identification of all trevally species is particularly difficult. The bigeye trevally is best identified by the gelatinous covering to the rear of the relatively large eye. There are white tips to the dorsal and anal fins and a small black spot on the rear edge of the gill cover. The bigeye trevally's breast is fully scaled which separates it from the giant trevally. Juvenile bigeye trevally prefer the tidal flats and can be quite common while large fish patrol close to deep drop-offs Reaching 80 centmetres.

Fishing: An avid lure taker, the bigeye trevally is fished near areas of fast water near reef gaps. Poppers work extremely well, with chrome slices, minnow lures and jigs also appealing. Smaller fish, can be sight fished on tidal flats. Lures, a rapidly stripped fly or fresh bait, that is kept moving will bring a strike and other fish also trying to get the lure. On a rising tide, these fish can often be on the inside of the reef edges.

Like all trevally, the fish should be bled and immediately iced. The removal of the red meat along the lateral line will make the taste more mild.

TRIPLE TAIL

Scientific name: *Lobotes surinamensis*. Also known as Jumping cod.

Description: The tripletail is a found in mangrove creeks, estuaries and inshore reefs which can reach 1 m and around 11 kg but is more common at smaller sizes. The elongated soft dorsal and anal fins which gives the resemblance of three tails.

The eye is relatively small and the mouth is also fairly small, finishing in front of the eye.

Fishing: The triple tail is a very strong fighter, and can also be a strong jumper.

The triple tail is commonly found near drop-offs in mangrove creeks or near structures in estuaries. Triple tails take lures well, particularly minnow lures, slices and jigs. They will also readily take fresh cut baits, pilchards or small live baits. The triple tail is excellent eating and many rate this species above barramundi.

TREVALLY, GIANT

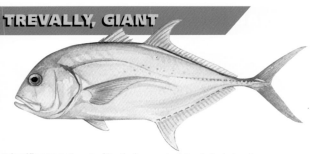

Scientific name: *Caranx ignobilis.* Also known as Lowly trevally, barrier trevally.

Description: The giant trevally is the largest of the trevally reaching 1.7 m in length and 60 kg which would be almost unstoppable on stand up fishing tackle. The steep profile of the head is typical of the giant trevally. There is also a small scale-less area on the ventral surface immediately in front of the ventral fins. A small patch of scales is generally found in the middle of this otherwise scale-less patch. There is no opercular (cheek) spot which is present on the bigeye trevally.

As giant trevally increase in size, they form smaller schools with the largest fish frequently loners. Large fish also prefer deeper channels between large reefs while smaller fish are found on tidal flats or on the edges of shallower reefs.

Fishing: Small giant trevally are one of the most challenging species for lure fishers in the tropics, with spinning near the edges of reefs, on drop-offs on tidal flats or sight fishing to individuals or small schools working well. Poppers are particularly attractive to these fish and can also be used as a teaser for fly fishers. Giant trevally also take minnow lures, large spoons and lead-headed jigs.

Rigs and Tactics:

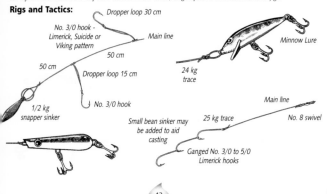

Dropper loop 30 cm

No. 3/0 hook - Limerick, Suicide or Viking pattern

Main line

50 cm

50 cm

Dropper loop 15 cm

1/2 kg snapper sinker

No. 3/0 hook

Minnow Lure

24 kg trace

Main line

Small bean sinker may be added to aid casting

25 kg trace

No. 8 swivel

Ganged No. 3/0 to 5/0 Limerick hooks

saltwater Species

TREVALLY, GOLDEN

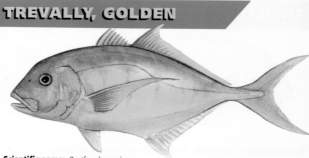

Scientific name: *Gnathanodon speciosus.*

Description: The golden trevally is also a large species reaching 1.2 m and 37 kilograms.

Juvenile golden trevally are striking and are often associated with large fish or sharks. They are a bright gold with vertical black stripes the first of which passes through the eye.

Larger fish lose the distinctive stripes and the eye is quite small. These fish are often quite silver when caught but flash yellow as they die and then are golden coloured, especially on the belly. A number of black spots are often present on the side, commonly near the tail but the number and size varies and they may not be present.

The most obvious feature of this species is that they lack teeth.

Rigs and Tactics:

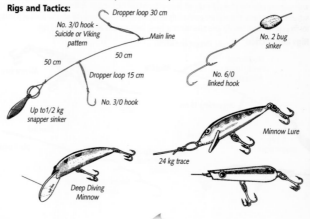

Dropper loop 30 cm

No. 3/0 hook - Suicide or Viking pattern

Main line

50 cm

50 cm

Dropper loop 15 cm

No. 3/0 hook

Up to 1/2 kg snapper sinker

No. 2 bug sinker

No. 6/0 linked hook

Minnow Lure

24 kg trace

Deep Diving Minnow

44

TREVALLY, SILVER

Scientific name: *Pseudocaranx dentex*. Also known as White trevally, skipjack trevally, skippy, trevally, blurter.

Description: A common schooling fish of cooler waters, the silver trevally is found in inshore areas but may be found near offshore cover. Juveniles are often encountered in estuaries and bays but larger fish can also be found in these areas on occasions.

The fins may be yellow and a narrow yellow stripe is often found on these fish but most fish are silver with a blue-green or darker blue, and dark bands may be present. The very similar sand trevally (*Pseudocaranx wrighti*) of central Western Australia only grows to around 800 g and has more prominent dark bands. The silver trevally can reach 1 m and more than 10 kg but fish of 2 kg are much more common and in most areas, a fish of 5 kg is noteworthy.

The mouth is relatively small, finishing well in front of the start of the eye and the lips are rubbery. There is an obvious black spot on the rear edge of the opercular (cheek) bone.

Rigs and Tactics:

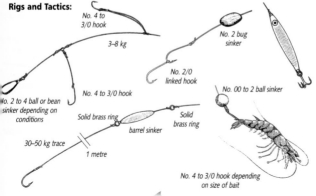

TROUT, CORAL

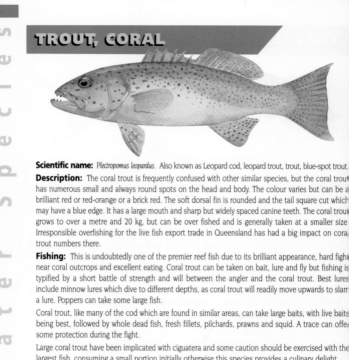

Scientific name: *Plectropomus leopardus*. Also known as Leopard cod, leopard trout, trout, blue-spot trout.

Description: The coral trout is frequently confused with other similar species, but the coral trout has numerous small and always round spots on the head and body. The colour varies but can be a brilliant red or red-orange or a brick red. The soft dorsal fin is rounded and the tail square cut which may have a blue edge. It has a large mouth and sharp but widely spaced canine teeth. The coral trout grows to over a metre and 20 kg, but can be over fished and is generally taken at a smaller size. Irresponsible overfishing for the live fish export trade in Queensland has had a big impact on coral trout numbers there.

Fishing: This is undoubtedly one of the premier reef fish due to its brilliant appearance, hard fight near coral outcrops and excellent eating. Coral trout can be taken on bait, lure and fly but fishing is typified by a short battle of strength and will between the angler and the coral trout. Best lures include minnow lures which dive to different depths, as coral trout will readily move upwards to slam a lure. Poppers can take some large fish.

Coral trout, like many of the cod which are found in similar areas, can take large baits, with live baits being best, followed by whole dead fish, fresh fillets, pilchards, prawns and squid. A trace can offer some protection during the fight.

Large coral trout have been implicated with ciguatera and some caution should be exercised with the largest fish, consuming a small portion initially otherwise this species provides a culinary delight.

Rigs and Tactics:

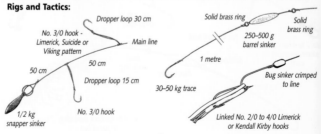

TROUT, CORONATION

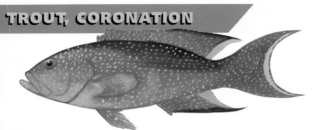

Scientific name: *Variola louti*. Also known as Lunar-tailed cod, fairy cod.

Description: The coronation trout is a beautiful fish which has vivid red or red-orange colouration flecked with yellow or red. The tail is distinctive with a sickle or lunar crescent shape and a distinctive yellow trailing edge. The cheeks and all the other fins are tinged with yellow on the trailing edge, especially the pectoral fins.

The coronation trout is quite common on coral reefs, but may be found on deeper reefs to 100 metres. It grows to 80 cm and around 3 kilograms.

TUNA, LONGTAIL

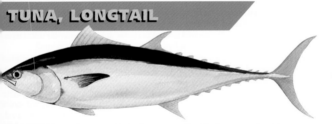

Scientific name: *Thunnus tonggol*. Also known as Northern bluefin tuna, northern blue.

Description: The name longtail comes from the light build to the rear half of this species, giving a narrow tail wrist and a slender outline. The pectoral fin is very short and finishes well in front of the start of the second dorsal fin which readily separates the species from yellowfin and bigeye tuna. This species is much more common in tropical waters but can migrate southwards in summer.

Fishing: In tropical waters, small longtails can form vast schools like mackerel tuna or bonito. These schools move rapidly and fish can be caught by casting lures or trolling lures or baits near the edge of the feeding school. Minnow lures, lead slugs or Christmas tree lures, feather jigs, spoons and flies all work well with larger fish preferring larger lures and a faster retrieve.

Longtail prefer inshore waters and although most are taken by anglers in boats, longtail are a highly prized land based game species. Specialised gear with live baits below large floats or balloons or high speed spinning can bring these speedsters to the rocks.

TUNA, MACKEREL

Scientific name: *Euthynnus affinis*. Also known as Jack mackerel, little tuna, kawa-kawa.

Description: The mackerel tuna is a highly prized lightweight game species which is caught in inshore waters or larger bays, harbours and large estuarine systems as well as offshore islands or larger reefs. The mackerel tuna can reach 1 m in length and 12 kg but is much more common at 2 – 8 kilograms.

The mackerel tuna has prominent wavy green lines in the rear portion of the body above the midline. The mackerel tuna is similar to the frigate mackerel but the first dorsal of the mackerel tuna reaches almost to the second dorsal while the frigate mackerel's first dorsal is short and widely separated from the second dorsal fin. The mackerel tuna has two to five dark spots above the ventral fin and more prominent teeth than the frigate mackerel which also only reaches 58 cm in length.

Fishing: The mackerel tuna is a schooling fish which feeds heavily on pilchards, herrings, whitebait anchovies, squid and occasionally krill. However, even when a feeding school is located, they can be very selective and difficult to entice to strike.

Mackerel tuna are mainly taken on fast trolled or high speed retrieved lures such as plastic skirted lures, Christmas tree lures, minnow lures, plastic squids, lead jigs and feather lures and spoons. The mackerel tuna will take live baits, fresh dead baits either cast and retrieved, trolled or fished under a float. They will more rarely take cut baits. Mackerel tuna are a frequent catch of high speed land based game fishermen.

Rigs and Tactics:

TUNA, STRIPED

Scientific name: *Katsuwonis pelamis*. Also known as Skipjack, skipjack tuna, stripey, aku.

Description: The striped tuna is a small, thickset schooling species which rapidly tapers at the rear of the body to a smallish tail. Sometimes misidentified as a bonito, but striped tuna lack the obvious teeth of the bonito and have no stripes on the upper flanks or back. Instead, the 4 – 6 horizontal stripes on the striped tuna are found on the lower flanks and belly. The area under and around the pectoral fin lacks stripes.

The striped tuna can reach more than 15 kg, but in Australia any fish over 10 kg is exceptional and the average size is between 1 and 6 kilograms. Schools of striped tuna can be massive and may contain hundreds of tonnes of fish. This species forms the basis of significant commercial fisheries in many countries.

GOLDSPOT TREVALLY (TURRUM)

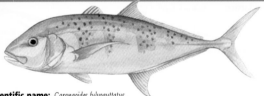

Scientific name: *Carangoides fulvoguttatus*.
Also known as Gold spotted trevally, yellow spotted trevally.

Description: The turrum is a largely tropical species that may move further south during summer. It is found in inshore waters and around shallow and occasionally mid water reefs. A number of species are known as turrum, especially in Queensland, but the true turrum can be identified by a number of features. These include the complete lack of scales up to the base of the pectoral fin whereas the giant trevally has a small oval shaped patch of tiny scales in an otherwise large scaleless area of the breast. The second dorsal fin of the turrum has between 25 – 30 rays while the giant trevally has 18 – 21. The turrum differs from many other trevally in only having a band of fine teeth in each jaw.

The turrum can reach 1.3 m and a weight of around 12 kilograms.

TUNA, YELLOWFIN

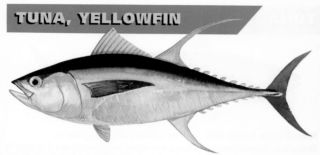

Scientific name: *Thunnus albacares.* Also known as Allison tuna, yellowfin or 'fin, ahi.

Description: The yellowfin tuna is a beautiful, powerful and challenging species which prefers warmer currents but may move inshore where deep water comes close to the coast. The yellowfin tuna is easily separated from other tunas by the scythe-like dorsal and anal lobes in adult fish. The pectoral fin is long and extends to the commencement of the second dorsal fin.

Small yellowfin have short dorsal and anal lobes, but have whitish bars down the sides which may disappear after death. The liver of yellowfin tuna is smooth as opposed to the ridged liver of the bigeye. The caudal keels (ridges) on the wrist of the tail are also dusky and never yellow as in the southern bluefin tuna.

Yellowfin tuna can reach more than 200 kg in other parts of the world, but in Australia fish over 100 kg are magnificent and most fish are between 2 and 50 kilograms.

Rigs and Tactics:

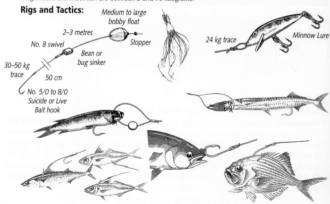

TUSKFISH, BLACK-SPOT

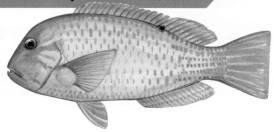

Scientific name: *Choerodon schoenleinii*. Also known as Blue parrot.

Description: A large tuskfish capable of reaching 15 kg and is found in sand and weed areas adjacent to coral reefs. The black-spot tuskfish is easily identified by the black spot which is found at the base of the middle of the dorsal fin. There is often a short, oblique purple bar set behind the eye and the tail is generally bright purple. The overall body colour is generally blue and the chin is blue-green or purple whereas in the blue tuskfish (*Choerodon cyanodus*) which is a smaller species, the chin is white or off-white.

TUSKFISH, VENUS

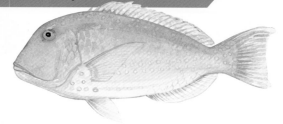

Scientific name: *Choerodon venustus*. Also known as Cockie.

Description: The venus tuskfish is a fairly small species, reaching 5 kg but most commonly seen at around a kilogram. They are generally bright pink along the flanks, being darker above and paler on the belly. There are numerous small white or blue spots on the body and the fins and tail are splashed with blue as are the lips and chin. The venus tuskfish prefers shallow to mid depth reef country and is found very close to reefs where it feeds.

WAHOO

Scientific name: *Acanthocybium solandri*. Also known as Ono, 'hoo.

Description: The wahoo is a long and sleek pelagic species which is capable of very fast movement i the water. Most wahoo in Australian waters are between 8 and 30 kg but they can reach 65 kilograms.

The wahoo is a solitary open water species which can be identified by the long and higher dorsal fin approximately even height. The dorsal fin starts behind the commencement of the pectoral fin while wit the Spanish mackerel it commences at the leading edge of the pectoral. The head is longer and mon pointed with the wahoo and the trailing edge of the tail fin is vertical compared to the forked tail of th other mackerels.

The wahoo has a number of prominent zebra-like vertical stripes along the body but these are les noticeable in some especially larger specimens and fade considerably after death.

WHITING, TRUMPETER

Scientific name: *Sillago maculata*. Also known as Diver whiting, winter whiting, spotted whiting.

Description: The trumpeter whiting is a common schooling fish with a preference for silty botto or deeper gutters of bays and estuaries. The trumpeter whiting is more commonly taken during th cooler months, especially on the east coast. The trumpeter whiting reaches 30 centimetres.

It is easily identified by having a series of irregular and disjointed brown blotches, spots or vertic marks. The similar eastern school whiting (*Sillago flindersi*) or southern school whiting (*Sillago bassens* both have unbroken vertical stripes. All of these species have a silver stripe which runs along th middle of the body.

WHITING, SAND

Scientific name: *Sillago ciliata*. Also known as Silver whiting, summer whiting, blue nose whiting.

Description: The sand whiting is a common species of inshore and tidal sandy areas. The sand whiting can reach 47 cm and around a kilogram. It is readily identified by the lack of a silver stripe along the side and the dusky blotch at the base of the pectoral fin. Large sand whiting are sometimes confused with bonefish, but all whitings have two dorsal fins while the bonefish has one.

A similar species, the yellow-finned whiting (also known as the Western sand whiting) (*Sillago schomburgkii*) reaches 42 cm but is only found from the Gulf of St Vincent in South Australia to Shark Bay in Western Australia. The yellow-finned whiting species lacks the dusky blotch at the base of the pectoral fin and is commonly taken on blue sardines, whitebait or small cut baits.

Fishing: A scrappy little fighter which gives a good account of itself for its size. The sand whiting is a terrific light line quarry and fine tackle will greatly increase the number of strikes. Use the absolute minimum weight to either reach the bottom or to keep the bait from swinging wildly in current or wave wash. Sand whiting will take a moving bait and a slow retrieve will attract fish. A long trace behind a small ball sinker is the preferred rig. As whiting have a small mouth, a long shank hook around size 6 – 2 is recommended. Either putting red tubing or a few red beads above the hook works very well.

Rigs and Tactics:

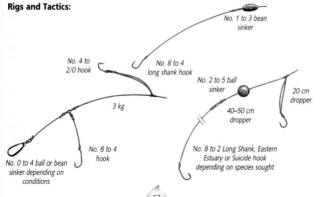

BASS, AUSTRALIAN

Scientific name: *Macquaria novemaculeata.* Also known as Bass, Australian perch.

Description: The Australian bass is a handsome fish which can reach more than 4 kg i[n] impoundments, but any fish from the rivers over 2.4 kg is an extremely noteworthy capture. Male[s] are smaller than females and a large male will be up to 1.5 kilograms.

The Australian bass is easily confused with the similar estuary perch. Even experts can confuse th[e] two species, but they can be most easily separated by the forehead profile which is straight or slightl[y] rounded in the bass and is concave or slightly indented in the estuary perch. Australian bass mus[t] have salt water to breed and the increased construction of weirs and dams on coastal streams ha[s] had a significant impact on bass numbers.

Fishing: The Australian bass is arguably the best light tackle sportfish of temperate waters i[n] Australia. They have a close affinity for structure and will dash out from their snag to grab a lure, ba[it] or fly and madly dash back into cover, busting off the unwary. While not as powerful as mangrov[e] jacks of tropical waters, they are spectacular sport in their own right.

Australian bass can be extremely aggressive, feeding on fish, shrimps, prawns, insects, lizards an[d] small snakes that may fall into the water.

Australian bass are more active at dusk, dawn or at night. Fishing on a summer's evening is almos[t] unbeatable, with surface lures or popping bugs on a fly rod producing spectacular strikes at dusk an[d] well into the night. Many lures work well and bass anglers are have massive collections of surfac[e] lures, shallow divers, deep divers, soft plastics, spinnerbaits and special lures in every conceivabl[e] pattern and colour. Many baits work well for bass, with live baits being best. A live shrimp or praw[n] drifted under a quill float will almost guarantee a response from any bass, but this includes very sma[ll] fish which may be gut hooked if the hook is set too late. Live fish such as poddy mullet also wor[k] well, as do grasshoppers, worms and live cicadas during summer.

Rigs and Tactics:

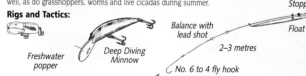

Freshwater popper

Deep Diving Minnow

Balance with lead shot

2–3 metres

No. 6 to 4 fly hook

Stopper

Float

CARP

Scientific name: *Cyprinus carpio*. Also known as European carp, Euro, common carp, koi, blubber lips, mud sucker. Lightly scaled individuals known as mirror carp and those with no or very few scales are known as leather carp.

Introductions are likely to continue through escaped koi carp from farm dams or poorly designed garden ponds. Carp are also introduced by foolish but well intentioned people who release their pets into waterways when they grow too large or the family goes on holidays.

Description: The carp has a relatively small, downward pointing mouth surrounded by two pairs of barbels, with the second pair more prominent. The first spines in the dorsal and anal fins are strongly serrated. Scales may be present, in rows and of a larger size, or almost entirely absent.

The decorative koi is a variety of carp and, if released, can breed to wild strain fish capable of much more rapid growth and reproduction. Carp can hybridise with common goldfish (*Carassius auratus*).

Fishing: Although much maligned, the carp is a powerful fighting fish, especially on light line. Carp are here to stay and in many urban areas provide fishing where little or none was previously available. They can reach 10 kg or more but are more common at 2 – 5 kilograms.

Carp can be taken on a wide variety of bait rigs, but coarse fishing techniques ele vate carp to a much higher level. The use of coarse fishing gear, rigs and baits such as corn kernels and maggots can account for big bags of carp. Carp take wet flies well and occasionally take lures intended for trout.

Carp should not be returned to the water but should not just be left on the banks to rot.

Carp are poor eating, although some people do enjoy them, in spite of their frequent muddy taste and large number of Y shaped bones.

Rigs and Tactics:

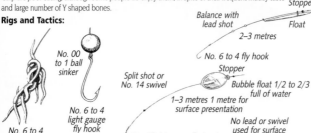

No. 6 to 4
Baitholder hook

No. 00
to 1 ball
sinker

No. 6 to 4
light gauge
fly hook

Split shot or
No. 14 swivel

1–3 metres 1 metre for
surface presentation

No. 6 light gauge fly hook

Stopper

Balance with
lead shot

2–3 metres

Float

No. 6 to 4 fly hook

Stopper

Bubble float 1/2 to 2/3
full of water

No lead or swivel
used for surface
presentations

CATFISH, EEL-TAILED

Scientific name: *Tandanus tandanus*. Also known as Tandan, freshwater jewfish, dewfish, freshwater catfish, kenaru, cattie, tandan catfish.

Description: A fascinating largely nocturnal species with smooth skin and a robust eel-like tail. The eel-tailed catfishes' intimidating looks mask a terrific eating and hard fighting fish.

The eel-tailed catfish possesses stout and poisonous spines on the dorsal and pectoral fins. The poison is stronger in juvenile catfish for, as the fish grows, the channel along the spine where the poison passes grows over and the spikes become less dangerous in animals over about 20 centimetres. However, the small fish hide in weeds during the day and can spike unwary waders. Immerse the wound in hot water and seek medical advice if swelling or persistent pain cause continued discomfort.

These catfish do not possess a true stomach, merely a modification of the intestine. The testes look like fancy scalloping edging and catfish mate in large excavated nests of up to a metre in diameter, which they aggressively defend.

COD, MARY RIVER

Scientific name: *Maccullochella peelii mariensis* Also known as Cod, Queensland Freshwater cod.

Description: The Mary River cod is considered to be found only in the Mary River. Has now been stocked into several Queensland Impoundments. Similar to Eastern cod, but more closely related to the Murray cod. They are more lighlty built than the Murray cod, especially near the tail and have heavier mottling patterns. Easily separated by the limited range. This species is at risk and should be returned regardless of the prevailing regulations.

COD, MURRAY

Scientific name: *Maccullochella peelii peelii*. Also known as Cod, goodoo, green fish, codfish, ponde.

Description: The Murray cod is the largest Australian freshwater fish, reaching 1.8 m and 113 kilograms. Cod grow an average of 1 kg per year in rivers and 2 kg per year in larger dams. Has prominent mottling on body, reducing towards a white or cream belly. Fin borders except pectoral fins are white. Differs from similar trout cod in having lower jaw equal or longer than upper jaw, more prominent mottling and heavier tail wrist. Murray cod also prefer more sluggish water than trout cod.

Fishing: Murray cod are the largest predator in many inland waters. They take large lures, especially deep divers cast to snags or drop-offs in larger, slower rivers or dams. Murray cod are now a legitimate target for keen fly fishers. Murray cod reward patience, as a lure repeatedly cast to cod holding cover, or to a following fish will often eventually evoke a strike. As Murray cod are ambush feeders, large or flashy lures often work best.

Murray cod are best known for taking a wide range of baits including live fish (where permitted), bardi grubs, yabbies, worms, ox heart and even scorched starlings. Murray cod are very good eating, especially under 10 kilograms. Anglers should only take as many cod as they need.

Rigs and Tactics:

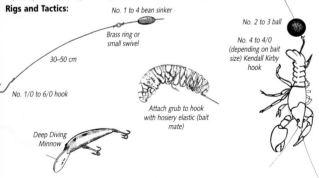

No. 1 to 4 bean sinker

Brass ring or small swivel

30–50 cm

No. 1/0 to 6/0 hook

Attach grub to hook with hosiery elastic (bait mate)

Deep Diving Minnow

No. 2 to 3 ball

No. 4 to 4/0 (depending on bait size) Kendall Kirby hook

Freshwater Species

GRUNTER, SOOTY

Scientific name: *Hephaestus fuliginosus*. Also known as Black bream, purple grunter, sooty.

Description: In the wild, sooty grunter can reach 4 kg and 50 cm, but in stocked impoundment such as Tinaroo Dam they can be considerably larger than this. This species has a reasonably lar mouth and the lips may be blubbery in some specimens. Colour can be extremely variable, from lig brown to black. Sooty grunter can be omnivorous and will on occasion eat green algae.

Fishing: The sooty grunter prefers faster water in rivers and can inhabit mid-stream snags in riffle In dams these fish are found around cover, especially fallen timber. Sooty grunter will readily take li shrimp or cherabin, worms or grubs. They will readily take a variety of lures including diving lure spinner baits, bladed spinners, jigs, soft plastics and flies. Sooty grunter fight well without jumpi and are undervalued as a sport fish by many anglers, partly because they are reasonably common many areas.

Sooty grunter are a fair to poor food fish which can be weedy tasting. Species such as barramur which occur in the same areas are much better fare.

Rigs and Tactics:

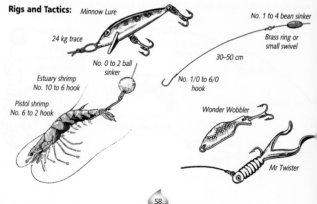

Minnow Lure

24 kg trace

No. 1 to 4 bean sinker

Brass ring or small swivel

30–50 cm

No. 0 to 2 ball sinker

No. 1/0 to 6/0 hook

Estuary shrimp
No. 10 to 6 hook

Pistol shrimp
No. 6 to 2 hook

Wonder Wobbler

Mr Twister

LUNGFISH, AUSTRALIAN

Scientific name: *Neoceratodus forsteri*.
Also known as Queensland lungfish, lungfish, ceratodus.

Description: The Australian lungfish is the most primitive of Australia's freshwater fish, which has remained unchanged for over 100 million years. The head is large and the eye very small. The body is brown and covered in large scales. The pectoral fins are large and paddle-like as are the well set back pelvic fins. The tail is extremely fleshy and though broad, is eel-like. The Australian lungfish possesses a single lung and can gulp air from the surface of oxygen poor waters, but unlike the African and American lungfish, it cannot survive completely out of water for extended periods.

PERCH, JUNGLE

Scientific name: *Kuhlia rupestris*. Also known as Rock flagtail.

Description: A handsome fish which can be distinguished by its preference for clean clear freshwater coastal streams. The body and base of the caudal fin is liberally speckled with dark spots. The lobes of the tail fin are generally white. The mouth is large and can take large baits and lures. This species has been severely reduced in range and number due to decreasing water quality in its streams. The jungle perch is a relatively small species, reaching 2.4 kg but rarely caught above 0.5 kilograms.

PERCH, GOLDEN

Scientific name: *Macquaria ambigua*. Also known as Golden, callop, yellowbelly, Murray perch.

Description: The golden perch is a deep bodied fish which becomes more heavily set as it gets large Fish over 5 kg resemble a football, with a tail and a small moderately tapered head with a distinctly conca forehead. The lower jaw extends slightly beyond the upper jaw.

The colour varies with the water quality, ranging from pale green to almost cream out of very muddy weste waters to deep green and with obvious golden overtones, particularly in the throat and belly regio There are two distinctive extended filaments on the ventral fins.

Golden perch are most commonly encountered in the 1 – 2 kg range especially in rivers. However, th extremely successful stocking in Queensland, New South Wales and to a lesser extent Victorian impoundmen has seen a huge increase in the number of 5 – 10 kg fish being caught with the odd fish to 15 kg being reporte

PERCH, SILVER

Scientific name: *Bidyanus bidyanus*. Also known as grunter, black bream, bidyan, Murray perc tcheri, freshwater bream, silver.

Description: The silver perch is a fine freshwater fish species, reaching 8 kg but most frequent encountered at between 0.3 kg and 1 kg, especially in impoundments. Larger silver perch becom omnivorous or almost entirely vegetarian, full of the green slimy weed which can seriously affect lu and bait fishing at some times of the year.

The silver perch has a small head and small mouth, but they take large lures on occasions. As the fis grows, its head appears smaller than its body, especially in dams where fast growth rates leave heavier body in larger fish.

PERCH, SPANGLED

Scientific name: *Leiopotherapon unicolor*. Also known as Spangled, jewel perch, bobby cod, nicky.

Description: The spangled perch is a small, aggressive schooling fish with characteristic pattern of rusty or golden brown spots over a generally brown or silvery body. The spangled perch can reach 600 g, but in some waters, hordes of fish of 50 – 200 g will consume any baits in the vicinity.

SARATOGA, SOUTHERN

Scientific name: *Scleropages leichardti*.
Also known as spotted barramundi, spotted saratoga, Dawson river salmon.

Description: The southern saratoga is similar to the gulf saratoga, but the mouth is slightly smaller and the large scales carry two or more red spots which form a vertical streak. The protruding lower jaw carries two small barbels near the lower lip. The pectoral fins are large and extend to the start of the small pelvic fins. It is much lighter through the body than the gulf saratoga and consequently weighs much less for the same length.

The saratogas belong to a family commonly known as the bony tongue fishes, which means that the bony mouth can be difficult to set a hook into.

The southern saratoga naturally inhabits fairly turbid streams, but they adapt well to impoundments and provide additional sport for keen lure and fly fishers.

Fishing: The southern saratoga is becoming an increasingly prized species for specimen fly anglers who value the challenge of spotting and landing this fish. They will rise readily to large surface flies such as the Dahlberg diver and fight hard and spectacularly. Saratoga will also take lures very well, especially surface lures or shallow running lures. Live frogs and unweighted shrimps cast near cruising fish are successful.

The saratoga is very poor eating and is much more highly regarded as a sport fish. The very small number of eggs (only 70 to 200) produced by a female means that each fish is valuable and should be carefully looked after.

Rigs and Tactics:

Freshwater popper   Minnow Lure

Fly fishing is successful

No weight to 2 ball sinker

No. 4 to 3/0 hook depending on size of bait

CHERABIN

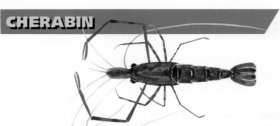

Scientific name: *Machrobracium rosenbergii*. Also known as cherubin, cherrabin, freshwater prawn

Description: A large freshwater and upper estuarine shrimp that is capable of reaching around 300 grams. It can be a deep translucent blue to a brown depending on the clarity of the water. Cherabin have a characteristic pair of very long, slender but remarkably flexible nippers that can be a dark brown or almost black. The nippers do not look like they can do much damage, but they can really give a painful nip. There is a similar species (*Machrobrachium australiense*) which is found in the Murray Darling drainage which reaches around 12 cm in body length and is often brown or translucent in colour.

MOSQUITO FISH

Scientific name: *Gambusia affinis*. Also known as Gambusia, eastern gambusia, gambies, Starling's perch.

Description: The mosquito fish is a small species, females reach 6 cm with males no larger than 3.5 centimetres. It is a live bearer, giving birth to miniature live young. The mosquito fish is a less colourful and flamboyant relative of the common guppy. The larger female has a prominent black spot at the rear of the abdomen where the young develop. The males have a large and prominent first anal ray which is called a gonopodium and is used to internally fertilise the eggs within the female. Under good conditions young mosquito fish can reach maturity within two months. Mosquito fish can rapidly build up populations, leading to large schools of these voracious fish which regrettably prefer foods other than mosquito larvae when alternatives are available.

MOUTH ALMIGHTY

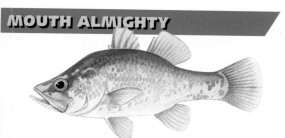

Scientific name: *Glossamia aprion*. Also known as Northern mouthbreeder, gobbleguts.

Description: An aggressive and very game species, the mouth almighty will try to eat any live food which is smaller than it is. The mouth almighty can reach 20 cm and 600 g but is commonly much smaller than that size. The mouth almighty has a pointed snout and a large mouth which extends behind the very large eye. A dark bar extends from the shoulder through the eye. The base colour may vary but is a shade of brown and can change rapidly when the fish is frightened. The mouth almighty is a mouth brooder, with the male taking up the eggs and holding them until they hatch.

RAINBOW FISH

Scientific name: *Family Melanotaeniidae*. Family includes: Blue-eyes, sunfish, rainbow fish

Description: Some of Australia's most colourful native aquarium species are included in the rainbow fish group, including the attractive honey blue-eye (*Pseudomugil mellis*) and the bright rainbow fishes. The group is recognised by a pointed and flattened snout, large scales, two closely set dorsal fins, the second of which is long and extends to the wrist of the tail and no scales between the pelvic base and the anus on the belly. The anal fin is also long and there is a membrane which joins the pelvic fin to the body of the fish. This group of fishes become more brightly coloured at spawning time, with males much more colourful than females.

Waterproof QUEENSLAND FISH GUIDE

THIS DEFINITIVE GUIDE TO QUEENSLAND FISH SPECIES AND HOW TO CATCH THEM

Containing accurate fish illustrations, descriptions, and diagrams of the best rigs to catch each fish, this book is an invaluable reference for any angler, fresh or salt water, wanting to identify their catch.

You will find Queensland fish from both salt water and fresh water.

When chasing fish in Queensland, you'll find the information you need to catch it and identify it in this comprehensive book.

Another great book by author, Frank Prokop.

Also available in this fish guide series: VIC, NSW and WA.

PO Box 544, Croydon Vic 3136
Telephone (03) 9729 8799

9 781865 130736